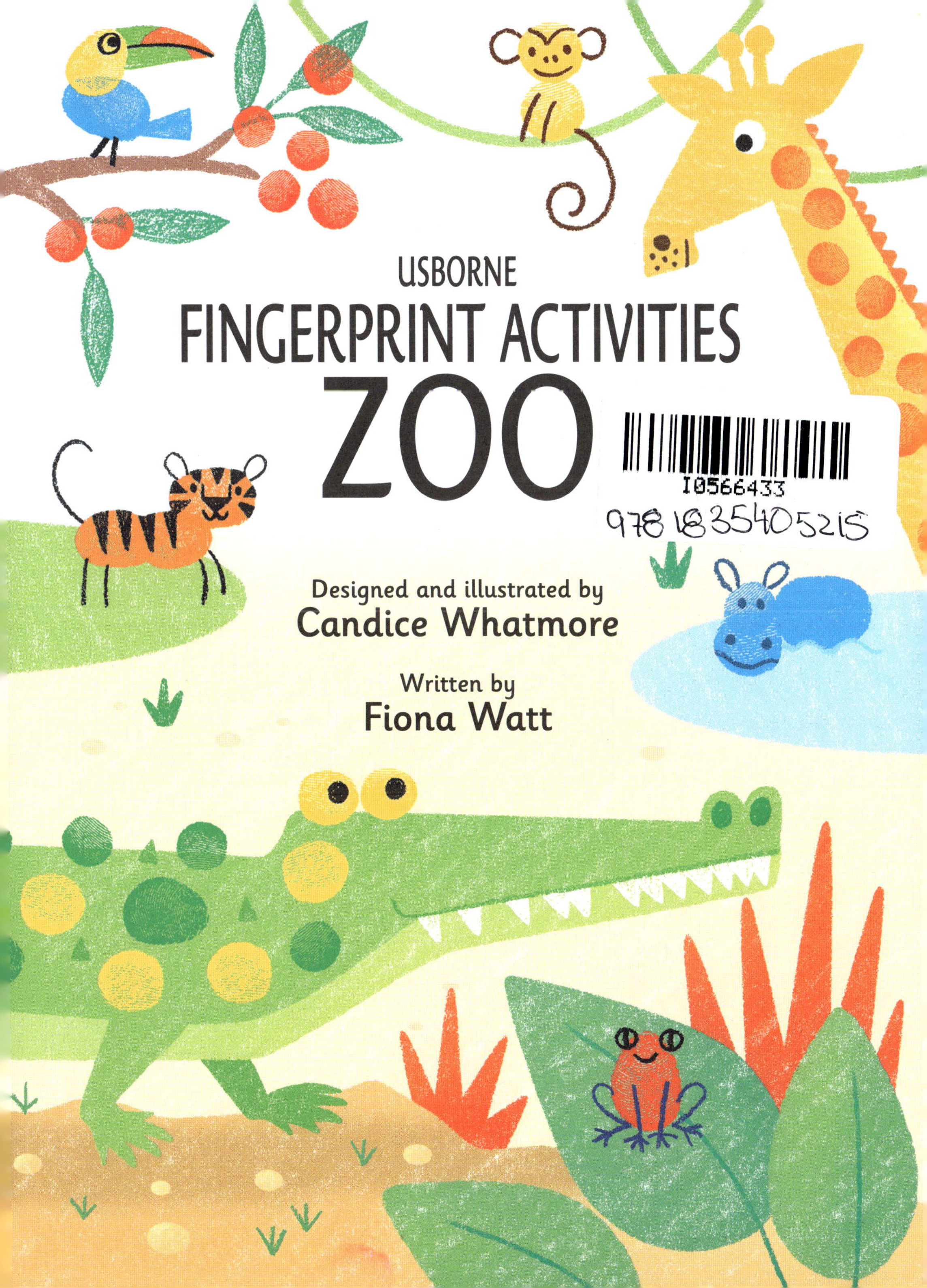

USBORNE

FINGERPRINT ACTIVITIES ZOO

Designed and illustrated by
Candice Whatmore

Written by
Fiona Watt

FINGERPRINTING TIPS

Press your finger onto one of the ink pads a few times to make sure you have a nice inky finger before printing it in the book.

Clean your inky fingers on a paper towel when you want to use a different ink. When you've finished printing, wash your hands with soap and water to get rid of any ink stains.

Try not to get the inks on your clothes or work surface as they may stain them. Don't lick your fingers – the inks won't taste very nice.

Use different fingers to make different sizes of prints. You can use the very tip of your finger to make a round print.

Fingertip

First finger

Thumb

Wait for your fingerprints to dry completely before drawing on them with felt-tip pens or crayons.

1.
2.
3.
4.
5.
6.
Use your fingertip and first finger to print more koalas climbing up the trees.

Print two eyes and lots of scales on the crocodiles swimming in the water.

NILE CROCODILE
Crocodylus niloticus
I'm Africa's biggest crocodile. I can be found in rivers, lakes and swamps in lots of African countries.

Add more tigers to the enclosure.

1. 

2. 

3. 

4. 

5. 

6.

Draw the legs and tail like this, for a tiger lying down.

Fingerprint blue and red noses on these mandrills. Then, draw nostrils and markings on their faces.

Add red bottoms
to the mandrills
that are standing.

Print more hippos wallowing in the lake.

1.

2.

3.

4.

5.

6.

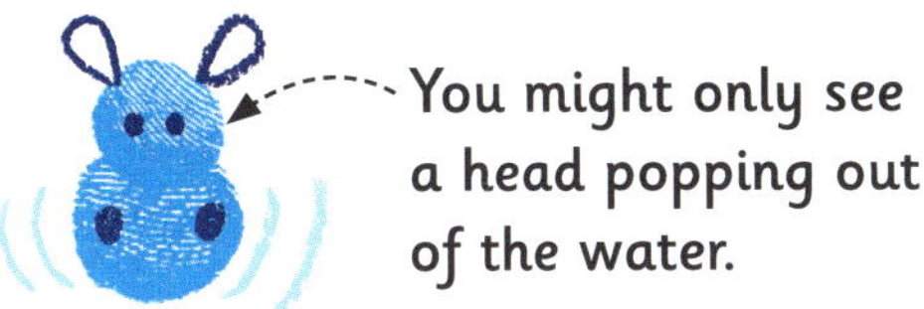
You might only see
a head popping out
of the water.

Fingerprint eyes and scaly patterns on these chameleons. Add leaves to the branches, too.

Add more meerkats acting as lookouts in their sandy enclosure.

Cover the giraffes' necks and bodies in fingerprinted spots.

1.
Print monkeys climbing over the cars in the safari park.
2.
3.
4.
Add people in the cars. Use your thumb to print a head, then draw a face and hair.

DO NOT FEED
THE MONKEYS

1.
2.
3.
4.
5.
Add parrots perching in the aviary.

Print pears and apples on the feeding tables.

Fingerprint furry yellow manes on the lions and add some lion cubs playing in the enclosure.

1.
2.
3.
4.

Add more gazelles running around their enclosure.

1. 2. 3. 4.

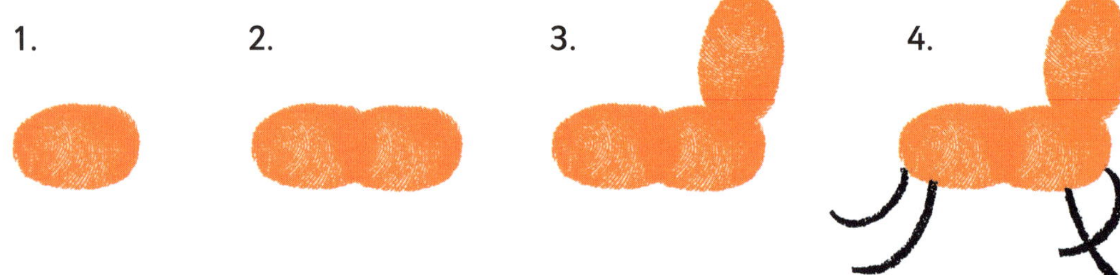

5.
6.
7.
Add an extra fingerprint
for a gazelle looking
this way.

Print more sea lions on the rocks or playing in the water.

Just print the head and draw a waterline for a swimming sea lion.

Add balls for
the sea lions
to play with.

Print faces on these orangutans.

1.
2.
3.

1.
Squawk! Add more toucans perching on the branches.
2.
3.
4.
5.
Print berries and leaves, too.

Use your first finger to print feathers all over the ostrich's body.

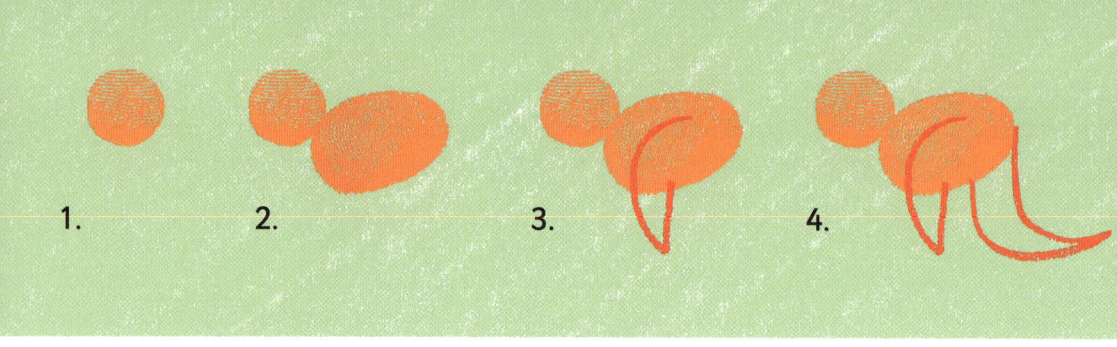

Add more wallabies beside the wallaby walk.

WALLABY WALK

Draw the tail and
leg like this, to make
a wallaby jump.

5.
6.
7.

These zebras need some stripes. Add rows of prints across their bodies.

Add a head, ears and a trunk to each of
these shapes to turn them into elephants.
1.
2.

3.
4.

Fingerprint stripes
along the lemurs' tails.

1.
2.
3.
4.
Welcome to the bat cave.
Add more bats hanging
from the rocks...

...and flying around the visitors' heads.

Fingerprint patches over the pandas' eyes. You might need to draw over the black eye again.

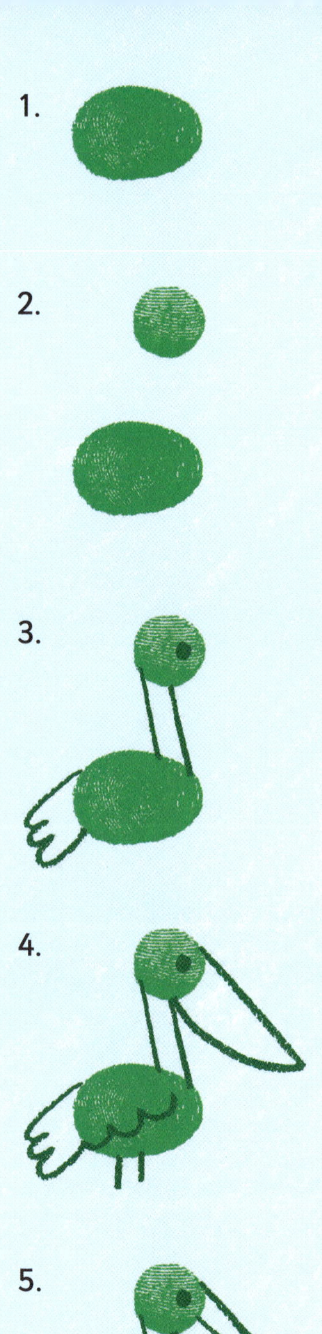

Use your fingertip for the heads and your first finger for the bodies to print lots of pelicans...

1.

2.

3.

4.

5.

...and flamingoes.

Fingerprint two separate humps on the Bactrian camels...
BACTRIAN CAMEL
Camelus bactrianus
We're two-humped camels. We come from rocky deserts in central Asia and western China.

...and two overlapping fingerprints for the dromedary camels' single humps.
DROMEDARY CAMEL
Camelus dromedarius
We only have one hump. We live in the sandy deserts of northern Africa, Asia and central Australia.

1. 

2. 

3. 

Print more penguins on the rocks...

Add visitors enjoying their visit to the penguin pool.

1. 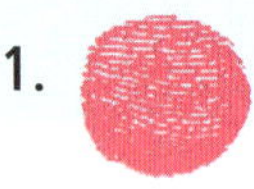

2.  

3. 

4. 

5. 

...diving into the pool...

...and swimming!

Add more curious raccoons playing in the trees.

1.

2.

3.

4.

5.

6.

1. 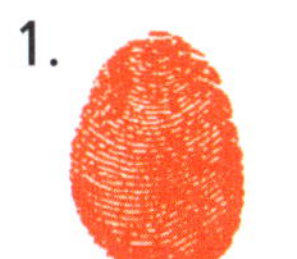 2.  3.  4.  5. 

Cri-ick, cri-ick! Fill the enclosure with more noisy frogs.

STRAWBERRY POISON DART FROG

Oophaga pumilio

I live in the rainforest in Central and South America where it's often warm and wet. I munch on ants, flies and other small insects. My skin is very poisonous so NEVER touch me.

Use your fingertip, first finger and thumb to add different sizes of spots on the cheetah's body.

1.

2.

3.

4.

5.

6.

Overlap fingerprints to create big, chunky, but friendly, rhinos.

1. 

2. 

3. 

4. 

5. 

6. 

1.

2.

3.

PETTING
ZOO

4.

5.

6.

1.
2.
3.
4.
Print a head on each snake's curly body.
EYELASH VIPER
I'm a snake from Central and South America. I hunt for small mammals, lizards and frogs, which I kill with a venomous bite from my long fangs.
CORN SNAKE
I'm a constrictor snake from North America. This means that I coil around my prey and crush it. I hunt for lizards, tree frogs, rodents, birds and bats.

BAMBOO RAT SNAKE
I'm a snake that lives in rainforests where there are lots of
places to hide. I slither amongst the leaves and branches on the
forest floor searching for frogs and small animals to eat.
GREEN TREE PYTHON
I'm a snake that lives in branches in tropical rainforests.
I hunt for small animals and reptiles, then squeeze
them tightly to kill them when I find them.

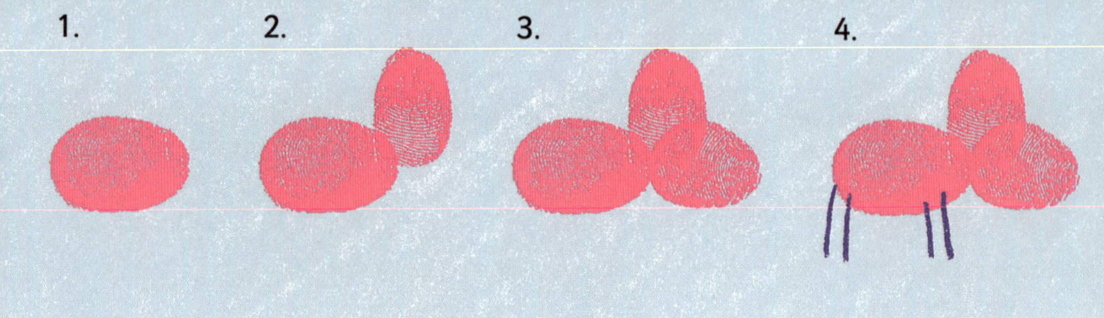

Add more warthogs cooling off in their enclosure.

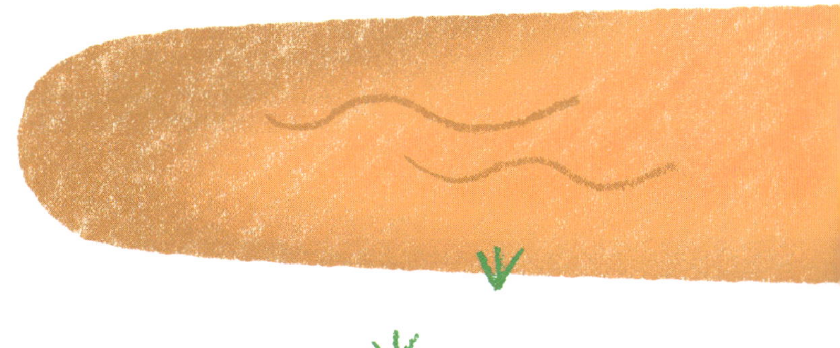

5.
6.
7.

Bloop... bloop... bloop... Fingerprint lots and lots of fish and turtles to fill the aquarium.

1.
2.
3.
4.

Shhhh! Don't wake the sloths. Add more sleepy sloths to the branches.

First published in 2022 by Usborne Publishing Limited, 83-85 Saffron Hill, London EC1N 8RT United Kingdom. usborne.com UE. First published in America 2022. This edition published 2024.